TEACH YOUR CHILDREN ART

A Handbook for Teachers and Parents

EARLY
·N°1·
YEARS

NIGEL MEAGER

Line, Shape and Drawing

NSEAD

VISUAL IMPACT PUBLICATIONS

Photography   Dave Daggers
Design   Andy Dark
Production   Nigel Meager

First published in Great Britain in 1996 by the
National Society for Education in Art and Design
in association with Visual Impact Publications.

NSEAD, The Gatehouse, Corsham Court,
Corsham, Wiltshire SN13 0BZ.

ISBN 0 904684 24 5

Imaging by Ideas into Print, Gower, Wales.
Printed in Wales by Pensord Press.

Thanks to the following for their help in producing this
book: Emrys Williams for the illustrations on pages 26–27,
Sally Basset, Bob Clement, Sophie and Joshua Coze, Lyndsay Edwards,
Rhys and Megan Edwards, Penny Hay, Julien Morton, Pam Rowden,
Josie Slee, Mike Smith, John Steers, Katie Thomson, Clement Williams,
Dunvant Infants School, Gladstone Infants School, Grange Primary
School, Gwyrosydd Infants School, Hendrefoilan Primary School.

Talking about drawing

2

Contents

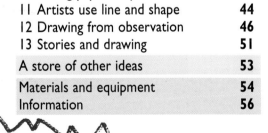

Why is art important?
Art and Education

Art is fun and enjoyable. Thoughtfully planned art experiences help young children's:

- personal and social development;
- language and literacy;
- mathematical understanding;
- knowledge and understanding of the world;
- physical development; and
- creative development.

This handbook is especially written for all those who want to help children aged from three to five years with their art. This includes parents and carers at home, playgroup leaders, nursery nurses, nursery and reception teachers and all adult helpers. It will provide them with an inspirational package of thought provoking ideas and practical advice that is based on sound educational principles. There is a rich and enjoyable mixture of activities that encompass investigative play, experimenting, talking, making and some ideas about teaching children basic art skills.

These activities are designed to be child centred. They aim to make the experiences, ideas and decisions of the children central, so that the art becomes meaningful for each child in his or her own terms. So, although the ideas are described in a step by step way, they are not 'how to make it' tips. Instead, the activities will empower children, stimulating a wealth of creative opportunities and a genuine expression of individual ideas and feelings. In other words I wish to avoid recommending projects that are only clever formulas for making art designed to please adults, where the end products look good but mean very little to the child.

understanding how we see. It can also help us to understand more about how artists use these same visual elements to represent the visual world and to express ideas and feelings - consider how distorting the shapes of features like mouths and eyes can make a portrait look disturbing, even horrific.

Taken together, these visual elements and the relationship between them is sometimes known as the visual language of art. When adults help children to focus on these elements through games, making activities or by talking, it enables them to:

- develop their visual perception, i.e. how they see the world;
- look at the world more carefully;
- learn words to describe what they see and feel;
- appreciate more about the work of artists, craftspeople and designers;

- open up to creative and expressive opportunities for their art; and
- make the most of the skills and processes needed for art.

In other words it encourages children to be thoughtful and discriminating about their perceptions, and to develop essential physical, creative and expressive abilities.

The visual elements of line and shape are the focus for this first volume of the 'Teaching Your Children Art' series. Colour and texture provide the focus for the second book in the series and three-dimensional form is featured in the third volume. Pattern, tone and space are part of both the second and the third books.

Drawing from 3-5

Psychologists who study child development have looked closely at the way children's drawings change as they grow older. If you are a parent, carer or work with children between three and five years of age, you may notice drawings that fit into one of the stages described on the facing page.

Because some children's drawing can develop in this way it can be dangerous for adults to make judgements about the quality of a child's drawing just based on whether it looks 'real' or not. Adults tend to draw things in predictable ways that children may struggle to imitate before they are ready. But this should not become a reason to step back from intervening in the development of a child's art.

All parents and carers will recognise that children need no prompting to draw - it seems both a natural and purposeful activity for them - and

Drawing outside

children's drawings will develop whether or not adults intervene in a conscious way. Consequently some adults may feel that it is harmful to 'interfere' with the natural development of children's drawing at such an early age. But, if you choose to step back now, at least for the time being, many of the rich opportunities that are described in the 'Teaching Your Children Art' series will be lost.

The message here is that although we need to be sensitive about the way children draw, teaching art in the organised but child-centred way described in this handbook allows us to enrich a child's experience of themselves and their world. And it is this which will promote your children's whole development.

1   Very young children make circular and rhythmical 'scribbles'.
2   Shapes emerge from the 'scribbles'.
3   Shapes are joined up and begin to represent different things.

4   A circle and two straight lines are used to make a figure and gradually children begin to add in eyes, mouths, arms and feet. They also combine circles and lines to make other images such as a 'sun' and 'spiders'. At this stage children often draw one circle to show both the head and the body of a person. Arms are drawn coming out of the head.
5   Children may concentrate on drawing a favourite object or person again and again. More details are included.

6   A variety of images are grouped on the page, often side by side.
7   The various images start to form more of a picture and children will often include extra ideas that do not refer to the main subject of the drawing at all.
8   Children begin to draw a picture in which all the parts relate to each other. They are able to make a good attempt at a more accurate record by drawing what they can see (see page 47).

11

Activities
Discovering lines

You certainly don't need to follow the exact sequence of activities as set out in the rest of this book. Why not dip in to the pages to try out some of the ideas? However, from page to page the suggestions do tend to get progressively more involved. You will notice that playing, exploring, experimenting and talking always precede the more detailed advice about the skills needed to make finished products.

Making imaginative drawings is a vital feature of children's development in their early years. Although children will draw imaginatively without prompting, adults can stimulate children by, for example, telling stories, joining in make-believe games or recounting what happened on a journey. Imaginative drawing should and will naturally feature in all young children's art (see page 51).

Artists and designers make good use of lines. For example, drawings are often made with lines, architects use lines when they draw a design for a building and lines can be an important part of a decorative pattern. Lines can describe edges and directions of movement and an outline can show the shape of an object. You only have to look around to see that the world is full of lots of different lines.

You could begin by making a collection of different 'lines'. In the photographs on the following pages, children are using ropes, cords, strings and cables which have different thicknesses, lengths and colours.

It is important to talk with children as they play. Think up different words to describe the lines. For example, you might ask questions like these:

An imaginative drawing, age 5

A straight line!

"Have you made a curved line? Can you make a straight line? I can see a wavy line - can you? Your line is all tangled and complicated. What about making a line with a bend in it? What kind of line are you going to make next? What do the lines remind you of?"

Children will enjoy working or playing with an adult and together you can make different 'pictures' with the lines on the floor or a table. Although it is easy to make simple images like faces and cars, why not just make an abstract arrangement of lines?

Talk some more together about the different lines you can see. For example, a fence might be made of lines or perhaps there is an aeroplane flying overhead making a line in the sky.

Exploring a basket of lines

Left: A face with curly hair

Why it is important to focus on lines:

- all young children use lines naturally when they draw;
- exploring and experimenting (see pages 14 – 19) will help them develop new ways of using lines in their own art;
- children can be helped to become aware of the world around them by looking for lines;
- talking about lines will improve a child's vocabulary; and
- they will understand how artists and designers use lines in many different ways.

Drawing lines

Work together with your children using a marker pen to draw lines on a large sheet of paper. Encourage them to draw different lines. For example, these might be straight, curved, wavy, long, short or they might twist and turn across the paper. Although more advanced children will be able to draw unusual lines independently, younger children will need your help. Again, talking about the different lines and using words to describe what the lines are like is a vital feature of this activity. Also, children could use different drawing media (for example, wax crayons, thick and thin felt pens, coloured pencils and chalks) to make even more lines with different characteristics.

Together, draw a line that moves in different ways as it travels across the paper. Perhaps the line could start very slowly and then speed up before coming to a stop. After a while it could bump along a bit

17

before climbing up a very steep hill and then tumbling down to the bottom. Next, the line could shake nervously across the paper before jumping and skipping to the end. You could make up a story together about what happens to the line. In the end children will be inspired to draw many new kinds of lines, for example: shaky lines, dotted lines, fast lines, broken lines and jumping lines.

Children should now work on their own. Encourage them to draw many different kinds of lines on their individual pieces of paper.

Natural lines 3

Exploring the natural world should be a feature of any programme that is designed to help children become visually aware.

- Go on a walk to hunt for different examples of natural lines. In the photographs, children were excited to see all the lines reflected in the pond and the lines that the branches and twigs of the trees made against the sky.
- Make an impromptu collection of the lines outdoors.
- Children can take photographs to remind them of what they discovered.
- Ask children to draw in a sketchbook some of the natural lines they find.
- Make a collection of the natural lines to take home or back to school or playgroup.
- Encourage children to arrange their collections of natural lines in different ways.

Children will soon realise that they can arrange the bits and pieces they collected into houses, people, roads, aeroplanes and such like. You could help them glue their arrangements onto a sheet of card or paper, suggesting that they could add other materials or pictures to enhance their imaginative collage.

Drawing natural lines

Hunting for natural lines

Drawing winter trees

- Ask children to look carefully at all the lines that branches and twigs make against the sky.
- Talk about these lines and ask questions about them.
- When children are focused on the task ask them to draw one of the trees, looking carefully at all the lines they can see.

If you are working with one child it is possible to talk that child through a drawing by repeating questions and suggestions about lines at regular intervals. This should prompt the child to look again at the lines they can see in the tree and then to continue to draw appropriate lines on their paper. The illustrated drawings on this and the facing page were made with black wax crayons. Suggest to the children that they should choose something to draw with that makes strong, clear lines.

24

These drawings are by children aged between four and five. They were left alone to draw after the initial discussion. The first drawing has a wildness that is instantly recognisable in the subject, the second shows that the child was looking carefully, the third is stylised but has a strong and complete character. Why not use a camera to make a photographic record of the tree to show with the drawings?

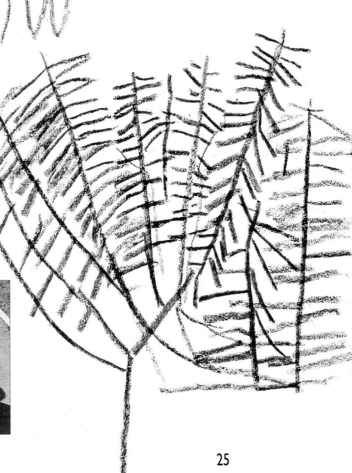

Talking about art

Talking about art with children is an essential part of 'Teaching Your Children Art'. Try out these questions and suggestions with children by talking about the drawings on this and the facing page.

- **"What can you see?"**
  It might be helpful for you to make a list (perhaps a mental list) about everything a child says. Read the list slowly back to the child and at this stage add some observations of your own. The shared description is a powerful foundation for a deeper conversation about the image.

- **"Show me different lines."**
  You could use the words to describe lines that came out of the preceding activities.

- **"Which part of the drawing looks the furthest away?**
- **Which part of the drawing is closest to us?**
- **What is happening?**

- **What is going to happen next?**
- **Show me part of the drawing you don't like very much.**
- **Show me your favourite part.**
- **Why do you like that bit?**
- **Now make a drawing of your own using some of this artist's ideas. You can draw some new ideas of your own."**

Drawings by Emrys Williams

27

Printing lines

Here are two different ways of helping children to make prints with lines. The first is called mono printing, the second is a form of relief printing. In each case it is important to talk about what to do; some children will enjoy being organised and work independently but you may need to remind others of how to work through each stage of the process.

Mono printing is the most direct of all printing processes. Young children can draw images in the ink with their fingers as easily as they can draw with crayons on paper.

To make a mono print:

- Children should roll or sponge some water based printing ink onto a flat plastic or formica surface (you can also experiment making mono prints with good quality ready mix paint).
- Encourage children to draw into the ink with their fingers, pressing down firmly to make bold lines. (You could also use sticks, feathers, sponges etc.)
- Help them to place a piece of paper carefully over the ink. Don't move the paper or the print will smudge.
- Ask them to firmly smooth the paper over the ink with the palms of their hands.
- Peel the paper off to reveal the print.

Peeling off a mono print

Drawing into the ink

Relief printing

Making a relief print:

- Use string or some of the twigs, stems and grasses that children have already collected (see page 21) or use lengths of string.
- Glue the materials to a piece of cardboard with a P.V.A. glue (this is a strong, white, water soluble glue) - children can use their fingers to apply the glue.
- Paint the surface of the card and string with the P.V.A. diluted a little with water and let it dry.
- Cover this in a water based printing ink - use rollers, sponges or brushes to apply the ink.
- Children can then place a piece of paper over the inky cardboard, pressing down firmly with the palms of their hands on the paper to make a print.
- Peel off the paper and peg the print up on a line to dry.
- Talk about the finished prints.

Have an old damp towel handy for inky fingers and use a damp sponge to remove any ink on tables or aprons whilst they are working. Soak all the inky brushes and rollers in a bowl, using warm water with washing-up liquid. After a while almost all the ink will rinse off under the tap.

It is important to repeat the procedure of inking up and printing, because children will then learn that most printing involves being able to repeat the same image again and again. Children and adults can also experiment by printing different coloured inks onto different coloured papers, or by using a range of colours to ink up the blocks in different ways. Also, after a day or so, the blocks may be dry enough to apply a second colour on top of the first. Children may need some help to make sure that the block goes back on to the right part of the paper, the correct way up. You can be relaxed about this though; a random reprinting can produce a lively end product.

Making a string print

Discovering shapes 7

When we are drawing we use outlines to describe shapes. It is often the shape of something in a drawing that allows us to recognise it as a representation of something real. Look back at page 26, where the artist has used different outline shapes to depict a balloon, train and boat. On page 13, a child has also used shapes to help construct quite a complex drawing. Shape is a key element in design of all kinds. For example, the use of shape by architects is a key feature in the way buildings look. You only have to look around to see that the world is full of different shapes.

Arranging simple shapes

Why is it important to focus on shapes?

- Children naturally begin to use shapes when they draw in order to represent different objects and people;
- exploring and experimenting will help them become aware of the richness and variety of natural and manufactured shapes;
- drawing around shapes and drawing different shapes is an excellent skill to practise as children learn how to write - they need similar manipulative and visual skills to form the shapes of letters;

A collection of shapes

- Cut out a number of simple shapes - for example, squares, triangles, circles, rectangles from thin coloured cardboard. Make the shapes different sizes and colours.
- Let children play with the shapes for a while and then ask them to pick out different squares, circles etc. They can go on to sort shapes into groups.
- Encourage the children to arrange the shapes in different ways. For example, can they make a face, a car or a house? Although this activity can be directed by an adult, more advanced children will develop imaginative ideas on their own.

- children will be helped to understand how to represent different parts of the subject they are drawing if they are encouraged to look for shapes; and
- an understanding of simple shapes is an important part of early work in maths.

Right: Arranging shapes cut out of card

Drawing around shapes

Children could draw around:

- regular shapes such as squares, rectangles, triangles and circles;
- more unusual shapes like ellipses and hexagons;
- irregular shapes cut from card;
- shapes made by cutting out images from colour magazines and gluing them onto card for reinforcement;
- the shapes of different manufactured objects collected from inside e.g. cutlery, toys, kitchen utensils, keys and shoes;
- the shapes of natural objects e.g. leaves, shells, flat stones and feathers;
- hands and feet;
- the shapes of their own bodies; and
- the shapes shadows make.

Drawing around shapes helps to improve the manipulative skills that are important for the development of both drawing and writing.

Above: Drawing around shapes. Right: Drawing around shadows

Cutting and tearing shapes

Start this activity by cutting and tearing irregular shapes with the children. You could close your eyes and tear a random shape from a piece of coloured paper. Put it on to a plain background. Prompt children to talk about what the shape reminds them of. Turn it and twist it and add other shapes to the background to stimulate fresh ideas. They can now make their own shapes, cutting with scissors or by tearing with their fingers, using different colours of paper and card. Before the cutting and tearing activity, children could have prepared paper using different processes to make different coloured or textured effects, for example, by painting, colouring with pastels or pens, marbling and printing.

Many children will need help to cut round drawn outlines. When children have a good collection ask them to play, arranging their shapes on a plain background to make different pictures of their own. Ask children to sort their shapes into different categories. For example, large; small; regular (like squares and circles) and irregular; shapes with curves; and shapes with straight edges.

Children can:

- tear irregular shapes;
- cut irregular shapes;
- cut round irregular shapes drawn on paper or card;
- cut round regular shapes drawn on paper or card;
- cut round outline shapes of objects drawn on paper or card; and
- cut round outline shapes drawn with templates.

Gluing paper shapes

Allow children to experiment using different tools to apply different types of glue, e.g. brushes, plastic glue spreaders, pieces of sponge, their fingers. They could use some of the shapes they made in the last activity and glue them to a larger sheet of paper or card.

The primary aim here is not to make a picture but just to let children discover more about the different properties of various glues. Organise the activity carefully so that children can explore each glue in turn together with different methods of application. Encourage the children to talk about what is happening when they use the glues.

Children will have a good collection of cut and torn paper shapes. They will have explored the idea of how to arrange this material into different pictures to represent different ideas. They will have also experimented with the glue and learnt a little about its properties and problems. Now they could add to their collection of shapes by cutting out images from newspapers or magazines. They could also cut out images from their own drawings. (Younger children may need help with cutting out.) Here is a more structured way of making a paper collage:

- Protect the table with a sheet of plastic (use thin polythene from a builder's merchants or DIY store).
- Use masking tape to make a line (like a boundary) that divides the table into two.
- The clean shapes and the background paper or card are placed on one side of the line.
- The glue, glue spreader, a damp rag for dirty hands and a small damp sponge to wipe off excess glue should go on the other side, the dirty side.
- You will also need an old magazine or a newspaper on the dirty side.

Making a paper collage

Ask the children to arrange some shapes on the background paper or card. Encourage them to make an imaginative picture. As their ideas develop on the paper you may be able to make up a story to go with their picture. This may not look particularly realistic but may mean a great deal to the child.

To glue the collage in place:

- Choose a shape and take it to the dirty side of the line, putting it on the first sheet of the magazine or newspaper.
- Put glue on the back of the shape. Encourage children to use small amounts of glue and to spread it over the edges of the shape. The glue spreader should go back into the glue container.
- Stick the shape on the background sheet.
- Wipe sticky fingers on the damp rag.
- Use the sponge to wipe away any excess glue.
- Turn to the next clean page of the magazine or newspaper, ready to put glue on the next shape.
- Children should repeat the process until their collage is finished.

Make it a rule that the glue, glue spreader, magazine or newspaper and damp rag should never cross over the line to the clean side of the table.

Children can add to their collage by drawing in extra details and images. When the project is finished talk about the collages - are there any stories to tell about what is happening in the picture?

You will need to work with younger children to help them follow the sequence and such a disciplined approach needs to be balanced by freer exploration of the materials (see page 40). However, once children are in control of their tools and materials they will be able to take more creative options. Both children and adults become frustrated if all that happens is that everything ends up in a sticky mess!

Right: An imaginative collage completed by drawing in pastel, age 4

11 Artists use line and shape

Children will find lots of different lines in this poster of a Paul Klee painting (right). They especially enjoy looking at abstract paintings which can help them to focus on visual elements such as lines and shapes (look back at page 8 for an explanation of the visual elements). Children will also want to talk about the different 'things' they can recognise in the painting. This painting is called 'Heroic Roses'!

In contrast, Rhys and Megan (above) are looking at paintings by the American artist, Roy Lichtenstein. They are excited by the shapes, colours and lines that make easily recognisable images to talk about. Why not borrow art books from a local library to show your children? Talking about art is a good alternative to reading a story and as a follow up children could go on to make abstract line paintings of their own.

Look out for the different lines and shapes in textile designs, domestic appliances, machines, cars, shoes, decorative patterns in the home, buildings, toys and anything else that has been designed and manufactured. Collect some examples of these shapes by taking photographs or cutting out images from colour magazines. Why not make a scrapbook of different examples of lines and shapes?

Talk about the shapes that artists and designers use. For example, the girl in the photograph (above) has discovered that Matisse has used different shapes for parts of the body. Other children (right) are drawing their own shape pictures inspired by a strange face made of coloured shapes by the artist Paul Klee.

12 Drawing from observation

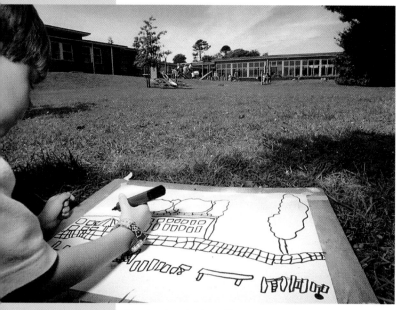

Drawing the school, age 5

The preceding activities will have helped children understand more about using line and shape in their art. This work should enable help more advanced children to draw from observation. In the following activity children are using lines and shapes to help them draw buildings.

The drawing of the house (see page 49) was made with a black fibre-tipped pen in a sketchbook. The drawing of the school was made with a black marker pen on A2 paper fixed to a drawing board with masking tape.

Before children begin to draw talk together about lines. For example, there might be a washing line, steps, drain pipes and lines in and around the windows - perhaps there is a line of houses in the distance, a line of roofs or telephone lines.

47

On a sunny day it is possible that some of the shadows make lines. It is so important to talk to the child you are helping before they draw.

You can talk with children about shapes and lines that can be seen and their position relative to each other. For example, you might talk in this way about the details of the back of a house:

"Why not start with the shape of the kitchen window? Now what can you see next to the window? The line of the drain pipe? Draw that in next. What is above the kitchen window? The shape of the bedroom window? Now draw that. Where would you put the shape of the door on your paper? Can you see anything else to draw that has a shape? What are you going to draw next?"

It is also helpful to suggest that children should start their drawing in the middle of the paper. In the illustrated drawings, both children began with the windows and added the outline of the building in later. As children draw you can continue to remind them about all the lines and shapes they can see, as well as prompting them to look again and include extra details.

Imaginative drawings are equally vital. Rhys drew the house at home from observation and the train at school from imagination (see page 9). Both drawings show his developing confidence with line and shape.

The activity of drawing, together with directed play and experiments with shapes and lines, is designed to develop the child's visual perception, offering a range of new creative choices.

Drawing the house in
a sketchbook, age 4

Telling a story in the nursery

Stories and drawing

The drawing opposite and the image on page 13 are imaginative illustrations for stories made up by children themselves with the help of an adult. Here is an example of how a story might start:

First, choose the characters for the story - you could ask, **"Who is going to take part in our story?"** Next suggest that the characters are going on a journey, **"Where are they going to go?"** What are they going to need on their journey? **"What should they pack in their suitcases or bags?"**

How are the characters going to get to the destination? **"By bus, by plane, are they going to walk or to fly and where are they going to stay? What will it be like?"** And what are they going to do when they get there? **"Is anything special going to happen?"**

Imaginative drawing, age 5

In the drawing above and on page 13, you can see a boy and a girl who went with their respective families on different holidays. The girl stayed in a

51

Imaginative painting, age 3

the same technique can be adapted to a story you are reading together from a book, or to a journey or event that has really happened. Children will invent wonderful characters and scenarios. They can of course also make imaginative paintings. More advice about painting with children is included in the second book of the 'Teaching Your Children Art' series.

On the left is a painting by a three-year-old girl who includes in her picture an imaginary cat called Meow who travels by aeroplane and train to the seaside in Wales to cook her owner a cabbage pie! There are seagulls, waves breaking on rocks, a beach with oil on it, an aeroplane, a railway track, a station and people waiting for a train, as well as Meow the star of the story herself! See if you can spot some of these elements in the painting. Imaginative drawings and paintings do not need to look realistic to be very meaningful for a child.

huge hotel with many rooms, the boy stayed in a caravan. The boy and his family travelled by train and the caravan was pulled by a car. Both the boy and the girl packed suitcases with the things they would need.

The story can be developed from here and continued over several days and weeks. Of course

A store of other ideas for working with line and shapes

We hope you have enjoyed reading about the ideas and looking at the illustrations and photographs in this book. However, there is no limit to the number of new ideas that experienced parents, playgroup leaders, nursery nurses and teachers can invent to help young children develop through art. This volume of 'Teaching Your Children Art' is really just a taster of some valuable child centred ways of working with line, shape and drawing. Here are a few more ideas:

- use the computer to make different lines and shapes;
- draw lines in compact sand, impress different shapes into sand;
- make clay tiles decorated with different lines and shapes;
- make plaster casts of natural lines and shapes imprinted into clay;

- make very large lines by coating tyres with paint and rolling them across large sheets of paper;
- make other kinds of lines by dragging or rolling different objects with paint on across paper;
- draw different lines and shapes in chalk on a hard surface outside;
- let some snails crawl through some food colouring and watch their trails become coloured lines;
- make lines in the dark with a torch (take a photograph with a long exposure);
- bend wire to make different lines and shapes;
- play games together, moving in different lines;
- make lines and shapes of objects e.g. arrange stones into different lines and shapes;
- make a pattern out of lines;
- make a pattern out of shapes;
- look at boundaries and edges; and
- look at lines and shapes on maps.

Materials and equipment

Here is a suggested list of the art materials and equipment you might need if you tried all the activities described in this book. If this seems a rather daunting list remember that children will enjoy working simply with paper and wax crayons and many of the recommended activities use basic materials.

For drawing:

Paper for drawing. It is helpful to have mixture of sizes and qualities available from A2 (420 x 594 mm) to A6 (105 x 148 mm). Cartridge paper is the best quality but is expensive; newsprint is much cheaper but tears and crinkles easily. A good compromise might be to use sugar paper, lining paper or photocopy paper for drawing. It is cheaper to buy paper in larger quantities from an educational supplier (see page 55 for a useful telephone number). Children can also draw on the back of used and scrap paper and card. This can be of excellent quality - why not make a store of scrap paper for children to use?

Sketchbooks. You can easily make an inexpensive 'sketchbook' by assembling a selection of paper that is held together by paper fasteners. Use a stiff card cut to the same size as the paper as a backing.

Drawing boards can be made from a rectangle of thin plywood cut to 425 x 600 mm. This will be large enough for A2 paper and provides a lightweight, flat, mobile work surface for drawing both inside and outside.

Masking tape. If you are careful, this tape peels away from paper without tearing and is useful for holding children's drawings to the drawing board.

Soft drawing pencils. You can buy thick soft pencils from educational suppliers, these are excellent for young children.

Washable black marker pens

Thin black fibre-tipped pens

Black wax crayons. These pens and crayons make strong clear shapes and lines that stand out. The resulting drawings can be easily photocopied if you want to keep a record of what children do or if you want to send copies to relatives and friends. Think about having different thicknesses of crayons and pens available.

Coloured wax crayons

Washable coloured marker pens

Washable coloured felt pens

Coloured pencils

For printing:

Card to use as a base on which to glue string or found material (see page 30).

Polythene sheeting to cover the table. Why not use thin builder's polythene that you can buy off the roll at DIY stores or builder's merchants?

Different coloured paper or card for the prints.

Water based printing inks

Something smooth and flat to roll the ink out on, e.g. plastic trays.

Rollers, sponges and brushes to apply the ink.

Rags

Pegs and a line to peg out the prints to dry.

Washing-up liquid, a bowl, hot water and old towels for cleaning up.

Aprons and/or old clothes.

For cutting and gluing:

Polythene sheeting to cover the tables (as above).

Masking tape

Paper and card - different kinds and colours.

Scissors

A selection of different glues, e.g. P.V.A. glue, a glue stick, non-fungicidal wallpaper paste.

Glue spreaders for P.V.A., glue brushes for the paste (children can also use their fingers!).

Old magazines and newspapers

A damp sponge in a tray

Old rags and towels

Drawing materials to add extra details to the collage.

You might also want a scrapbook and a large folder to keep some of the photographs and art work.

A wide range of **Crayola**® products are stocked in supermarkets, newsagents and toy shops. We have also prepared an information sheet that lists suppliers of art materials to schools, nurseries and playgroups. If you would like a copy of this free fact sheet please telephone **Crayola**® on **01234 360201**.

Information

NSEAD

The National Society for Education in Art and Design is the leading national authority in the United Kingdom, representing every facet of art, craft and design in education. For further information, write to:

NSEAD, The Gatehouse, Corsham Court, Corsham, Wiltshire SN13 0BZ.
Tel: 01249 714825 Fax: 01249 716138

The NSEAD has also published other books written by Nigel Meager that help primary school teachers teach art. **Teaching Art at Key Stage 1** costs £11.95 and **Teaching Art at Key Stage 2** costs £16.95, both prices include postage and packing – you can order these books by telephone on **01249 714825** or by writing to the NSEAD at the above address, enclosing a cheque or order.

Look out for the next two books in the 'Teaching Your Children Art' series. **Teaching Your Children Art, A Handbook for Teachers and Parents, Early Years No. 2, Colour, Texture and Painting.**

Teaching Your Children Art, A Handbook for Teachers and Parents, Early Years No. 3, Modelling, Constructing and Form. It is expected that both these books will be published by the summer of 1997. They are also intended for teachers and parents of children between three and five years of age. Contact the NSEAD or **Crayola**® for details.

The NSEAD publishes a free comprehensive book list of over 200 publications about art education and teaching art.

Binney & Smith (Europe) Ltd.

Binney & Smith (Europe) are the pre-eminent supplier of children's colouring and associated art materials. **Crayola**® products offer the very best quality and performance across a wide range of educational art activities. All **Crayola**® products are innovative and are designed to stimulate the creative development of young minds whilst providing lots of fun. Telephone: **01234 360201** for more information about the **Crayola**® product range.